My Wedding Dress

poems by

Heather Corbally Bryant

Finishing Line Press
Georgetown, Kentucky

My Wedding Dress

Copyright © 2016 by Heather Corbally Bryant
ISBN 978-1-63534-066-2 First Edition
All rights reserved under International and Pan-American Copyright Conventions.
No part of this book may be reproduced in any manner whatsoever without written permission from the publisher, except in the case of brief quotations embodied in critical articles and reviews.

ACKNOWLEDGMENTS

"After the First Lie" was previously published in *Lottery Ticket*, Parallel Press, University of Wisconsin-Madison Libraries, 2013.

Publisher: Leah Maines

Editor: Christen Kincaid

Cover Art: Heather Corbally Bryant

Author Photo: Heidi Lynne Photography

Cover Design: Elizabeth Maines

Printed in the USA on acid-free paper.
Order online: www.finishinglinepress.com
also available on amazon.com

Author inquiries and mail orders:
Finishing Line Press
P. O. Box 1626
Georgetown, Kentucky 40324
U. S. A.

Table of Contents

Walking the Neighborhood 1
Yellow Dahlias 2
Sitting on a Bench, Bellefonte 3
The Return Trip 4
Lightning 5
Holding me Underwater 6
Rainy Saturday Night 7
Signing Papers 8
The Courthouse 9
History 10
Socks 11
Vase 12
Yom Kippur 13
Phone Call 14
Tilt-a-Whirl 15
Separated 16
Splitting 17
My Husband's Movers Are Coming 18
Flies 19
Intake, Domestic Relations 20
Apology 21
Iconography of Daily Life 22
Marriage, One Month 23
Hearing 24
The First Dream 25
Requiem 26
Dissolution 27
Log Cabin Quilt 28

Rotting Potatoes	29
Burberry Shirt	30
Ritz Carleton Bar, Boston	31
Sidewalk, Ann Arbor	32
A Café near Chartres	33
Dancing School	34
Driving to Lewisburg	35
Jet Trails	36
Blood Tests	37
November	38
Twenty-Three Years and One Month	39
Mockingbird's Song	40
Shadow Builders	41
Reclamation	42
The Bucket	43
After the First Lie	44
Weeping Cherry Tree	45
Oysters	46
Detrimental Reliance	47
Plane Trees	48
My Wedding Dress	49
Trash Day	53
Spode	54
The Nightmare	55
Sleigh Bed	56
Leaving the Forest	57

For All of the Kind Souls Who Helped Me Find My Way Back

Walking the Neighborhood

This humid summer Sunday morning makes me long
For clarity—my husband and I talk as we walk
Through our still-sleeping neighborhood—
Well-tended, closed, chemicals sprayed on every lawn.

When we reach the corner where we usually keep going,
You say you want to turn around, your voice sharp as you
Complain it is always the same conversation with me,
My repeating anxiety someone will appear and steal

You away from me; at that moment I know the truth:
You are hiding everything valuable from me.

Yellow Dahlias

Here I am in the anteroom of my attorney's office—
Here because my husband of twenty-three years
Has committed adultery for at least the fourth time—

He is flying back east, calling me to say he will
Be landing soon. When will I be home to greet him?
My tears blur a glass vase of dahlias, yellow blossoms

Spilling color into the room, a bouquet stilled from
Summer. My mind clears this September morning:
He has forfeited any rights to whether he will stay or go.

Sitting on a Bench, Bellefonte

I blink away brightness. It is warm for autumn.
A bumblebee swarms close, sucking nectar from a red
Geranium. When the insect comes near, I swat it away;

An elderly man stops to ask me if I would like to buy
A purple prayer flag—no thank you, I say—not today—
I no longer crave totems of hope; the spell is

Broken; I no longer need to stand so close beside
The flame that burns my face—I no longer have to watch
As my husband strikes a match to kerosene,

Lighting a bonfire destroying the remnants of our life together.

The Return Trip

My husband texts me thirty-two times in one hour.
I refuse to answer the phone; that night in bed, my
Husband also apologizes for 'any pain' what he calls

'The situation' might be causing. Always the passive
Construction, as though he has no control over anything
That might befall him—I am disgusted—he compliments

Himself on having done his own dirty laundry—but
Even that task he cannot complete: I find his filthy socks and
Underwear wadded on the floor beside the washing machine

The next morning, he is already off to his new life.

Lightning

Today, you say, we are married, but you have no idea how long
That will last. You are confused, trying to think things
Through. Your girlfriend seems promising, but it is too early to

Know for sure—you've only just had your first date, after all—
When I listen to my husband speak these words, I no longer know
Who he means when he says 'we'—this lightning bolt, you call love

Struck this summer—even you do not understand what is happening
To you—you cannot fathom how lightning could have struck

Not once, but twice—I say it is easy to attract electricity when
You are standing naked in an open field during a thunderstorm.

Holding Me Underwater

Like an exquisite logician, my husband splits syllables—
He insists he is not having an affair; he only slept fully
Clothed on his side of her bed, an imaginary line drawn

Down the middle, separating man from woman, and
This he expects me to believe as an important truth—
Damns me for doubting his word, for even considering

The possibility he has anything to explain.
Either he has gone insane, or he knows no shame.

He aims to pull me down with him, holding
My head beneath water so no one hears me scream.

Rainy Saturday Night

My husband and I have made an arrangement, of sorts—
He will sleep in the basement and I will
Stay upstairs in our maple slatted bed, the one we bought

On our third wedding anniversary, where we conceived
At least seven pregnancies—more than half did not keep.
Before I go to bed that night, I ask if there is

Anything that would persuade him to stay—but he only shakes
His head as though mute, he cannot speak a word. I
Creep under the covers till the rains come—first with thunder

And then lightning flashing through the green curtains.

Signing Papers

Eight o'clock, on a blue-skied Monday morning—I drive
Ten miles down a highway to sit across the table from my
Attorney—my hands shake as I sign documents

Naming myself 'the plaintiff,' my husband the 'defendant'—
Petitioning to end our marriage owing to irreconcilable
Differences. Walking to the marble-columned courthouse

Clears my head. I know what I have to do and why, for the first
Time in years, I can hear the truth whispering
In my ear, telling me that it is already far past time to leave.

The Courthouse

I stand beside my attorney while she writes a check
To begin divorce proceedings. Someone behind me
Is sobbing, a woman I believe—I step away, so as not

To intrude on her privacy—but she begins to talk,
Anyway as if to the air, to anyone who is there—'a month
Ago,' she says, 'I thought my life was perfect—and now look

At me'—I nod my head as if to say I know exactly what you mean.

History

Holding your hand as blood poured out of me after giving
Birth—your face stern at my father's grave—
Your first smile at our last child, our son—so hard-won—

Your shoulder I cried on, for better for worse—you with
A tape measure sticking out of your pocket—measuring
Our houses, five in all, both old and new—your expensive black

Pen steadily signing hundreds of documents we've
Accumulated together—for richer for poorer, for better
For worse—in sickness and in health—now all shredded

We now part, we who promised only death would us part.

Socks

Lately, my husband appears childlike, on a different
Plane—trying to hug me, incessantly, the wife
He says he still loves; I run to escape his clutches.

He has only been gone minutes before he reappears—
Wondering if I can help him find the mates to all his
Missing socks, the ones I stupidly must have lost.

Vase

My husband begins to pack—
Not wanting to take this or that, his voice filled with false concern—
He insists he wouldn't want to select anything that has particular sentimental

Value—not the cutting board, nor the cookware we received as wedding gifts.
He simply fails to see that everything here has meaning

For me—marriage in the end comes down to daily objects of love.
When I cry, he orders me to 'Calm down' when it is really quite the other way
Around—I dare him to take the Lalique perfume vase he gave me for a wedding

Present before I smash it into a million little pieces; surprisingly, he does as I ask
Wrapping the opaque glass carefully in yards and yards of tissue paper,
Destroying the evidence of what once might have been called love.

Yom Kippur

Saturday afternoon on this Day of Atonement, and prayer
I hear my own voice inside my head instead of a god.
I myself can clear the air swirling around me.

Fingers unsteady, I place a call to my husband's girlfriend's
Mother; my attorney told me I need to explain I was not involved,
I did not know they were together when I invited her family
Into my home; that we, my husband and I are

Divorcing. My voice catches in my throat as I imagine my father
Looking down at me, hearing the word he so feared;
Her mother's voice on the phone saying, 'your husband, we would
Like to kill him,' echoes through our empty master bedroom.

Phone Call

Hearing my husband's voice these autumn days when I am in such a daze
Is disorienting at best—behind his closed door in our basement
He is constantly on the phone with his lover and our closest

Friends. I try to stay away, but there are times when I find
Myself there, walking down the hallway of my house too, for, to borrow
One of his phrases—both our names are on the deed—a legal problem

For me now. We have purchased everything jointly: I should have questioned this.
I hear laughter, giddiness, joy as he tells our best friend, the man who stood with
Us at the altar, *how beautiful she is—how he can't wait for him to meet her.*

My husband sounds like the Cheshire cat who has trapped his mouse, his first
Wife, in the corner while he sings his jolly song, wanting me to play along.

Tilt-a-Whirl

I am at the top of a rollercoaster ride, looking down
Below to where I know we are going—my stomach
Somersaults in fear, just as it always does moments

Before beginning the descent—the instant whether
You don't know whether you will go up or down, or
Whether you will be able to hang on tight enough

Before you fly over the edge—I am on a ride with my
Kids screaming not in joy but in terror, crushing
My sunglasses with my bare hands—I do not have

Any idea where or how or when we will land.

Separated

I walk downstairs in relief that I will not have to see my
Husband this morning—he has agreed to sleep at his new
Place—I can breathe a bit easier today, at least knowing

My life will be my own, if difficult—I hear a rustling
Coming from the room he claimed as his study—the place
We were never able to share—I jump when I realize

That he is sitting there at his desk, as though nothing out of the
Ordinary has happened—when I ask him why he is here, he
Explains that he wanted to say 'good morning' to our children,

Also, he forgot a few things. When I ask him to leave, telling
Him that he is trespassing, he screams that he will do *No
Such fucking thing,* he reminds me this is his house too,

Nothing, not even a court order, will keep him away.

Splitting

Last ditch effort—my husband wants to try one more marriage
Counselor—though years before, he's said no, and the first
One I found in the yellow pages didn't see a problem with my husband
Leading not one but two lives—so I have reluctantly agreed to see a second—
This gentle man is double-booked, but he takes us on—a couple in
Crisis he said, that's the first time I've heard that word spoken aloud.

He wants to see us separately, first, then together—we make
Arrangements. My husband calls me from the parking lot because
He is lost, can't remember the guy's name or address. I go

On my own—The man asks an open-ended question—
'How would you describe your marriage today?' I start talking
And I don't stop for almost fifty minutes. The doctor nods, listens,

Lets me speak unimpeded—just before our time is up, he finally
Interrupts me long enough to say he has just one thing to ask,
He emphasizes that there is no need for me to respond in any way

That afternoon, just something for me to think about on my own
For the next few days: Have my ideas or feelings ever been taken into
Account in this marriage? For me, that question has one answer.

My Husband's Movers Are Coming

On this September morning, coming towards my favorite time of year,
The air still blue and clear, but no longer suffocating—my husband's
Movers are coming to remove a portion of our accumulations of a quarter

Century together. I leave early to get to my classes on time; when I
See my husband's number come up on my phone I simply let it ring.
I have nothing left to say to him—his last brutal words still scream

In my head, *Go fuck yourself, because no one else will ever want to.*

Flies

I come home from my classes deliberately late—so that there would
Be no chance that I could somehow run into my husband and his
Movers. I circled our block twice to make sure the truck was gone.

But when I see that the front door has been left
Wide open for all to see the devastation
Within, I park on the circle and step inside to see what I can

Salvage. We had not formally agreed on what
He would take, mostly because we were barely able to speak
With one another by our most miserable end.

All I can see is a chair missing, a printer lifted. Whole rooms emptied.
Around me everywhere flies buzz, let in by his carelessness.

I can remember from biology class that flies are drawn to carcasses,
To what has recently died.

Intake, Domestic Relations

The temperature shoots into the nineties on this Wednesday
Afternoon, some people call this September day Indian Summer—
I sit across from a woman who types in the numbers of mine

And my children's life, of what it will cost my husband to support
His wife, and his sons and daughter—this fairy godmother sits
And enters a table of figures, printing out reams of paper from

Her computer, to make some repair for the injustice he has
Set into motion—making it possible for me to buy groceries
And gas to keep our life as intact as it can be, under the circumstances,

While my husband buys plane tickets, and makes hotel reservations,
Arrangements for what he refers to as his wonderful new life.

Apology

When I was twenty-two a married man invited me for a drink or two—
I accepted his invitation—the bar he selected was smoky, musty, and loud—
Neither of us could really hear what the other was saying—he put his

Hand over mine and I saw his gold ring flash in the darkness—
He was my boss, I thought this was all about business until he kissed
Me in the parking lot—I was too young to know that things like this

Did not only happen in the movies—when he called the next time,
I said I was busy—later I met his wife at a party, full of pregnancy with
Their first child—I knew enough to run away as fast as I could—

Almost thirty-years later, a woman half my age sends me an apology—
She is sorry she says, sorry for any hurt she may have caused—
I do not write her back; there are no words for what has happened

To our marriage—home wrecker is too clichéd a phrase, and yes, my
Husband should have known better, but she knew what she was doing.

Iconography of Daily Life

Looking around our house, I see everything carries a memory—
A blue glass perfume bottle my husband brought me from Stockholm,
The apple print with one slice missing that we bought together

At a gallery on the Quay D'Orsay on a sunny Paris October afternoon—
The trip we took after our first reconciliation—the hanging dyed
With berries from Maine in the back hallway, the one you had

Specially commissioned just for me with blues, greens, and purples
From the island where we spent our honeymoon—the photograph
Of us together, your arm around me beside the Cape Hatteras ferry.

Marriage, One Month

We had a huge fight that hot August night, so bad I could not
Even write about it in my journal—that's when I tried to stop
Feeling behavior that I knew was too painful to accept—

I had misplaced the keys, or something, my husband had been
Drinking heavily—I wanted to leave—when I told him he could
Find his own ride home he threw the ring of keys at me shouting

'Go fuck yourself'—I closed my mind that sweltering summer evening.

Hearing

For many years, I have listened, loved, and tried my best
To understand this wild creature of a man who has reached
Inside and plucked the heart right out of me—all the while

Saying everything is my fault—as I listen to him squabble
Over pennies at our hearing—he has already removed his
Paycheck from our bank account—I realize that whatever

Doubts I ever had have been supplanted, replaced—before
I asked him to leave, I bought extra food so that I knew our
Children would not go hungry—I can no longer count the

Number of promises he has doubled back upon, times he
Has given me his word, only to take it away again—and only
Then do I begin to see that what he says no longer matters—

Not in the least as he glares at me while I stand beside my lawyer.

The First Dream

Last night was one of the first times I have remembered a dream—
At least since this nightmare in my life began—I am beginning to
Understand how Sylvia Plath could not bear it when her husband

Said he might love another woman better than her, so convinced he
Was that his pleasure took precedence over hers—I have so many
Questions for my husband, ones I know I will never ask—what about

All those years we shared, the children I bore, the pregnancies we lost
Together—before he said he no longer knew what the future held
In store—nothing is as it was, he says, nothing—he owes himself

This one last chance at whatever happiness he could never find
Before—I wish he would have once said he was unhappy, just once,
Before he unleashed this terrible surprise upon all our lives.

Requiem

Music throngs like a gong through my head, like a dirge,
A sad sound echoing all that went wrong through all
The years we lived together, all those months that I

Tried to love my husband, and he could not find what he said
He wanted with me—just now he believes he has found
The love he could never picture before—and so he has

Set in motion the actions to bring our lives crashing
Down around us, one wrecking ball at a time, as I close my eyes
Against the pain; I repeat the words there will be love again.

Dissolution

Before I go to sleep, I think of all the words in existence to pronounce
The end of a marriage—dissolution, equitable distribution, divorce,
Decree nisi, and annulment, perhaps the most hypocritical one of all—

I think of how many of them derive from the same root, how all they
Indicate an undoing, an unraveling of promises made, vows reversed—
I have a flash of memory to our younger selves—I am standing alone

In our kitchen when I close my eyes against the poignancy of recall—
My husband holding both my hands and standing at the altar, pledging
His troth to mine, each to the other—I can still hear his loud voice

Echoing: forsaking all others, until death us do part.

Log Cabin Quilt

All through that chilly winter my husband hid from me, gradually
Withdrawing day by day—every morning I awakened to an empty
Bed, half cold with loss, he was already at his computer, working overtime,

Was what he said—but really typing love letters to a virtual stranger,
A woman he eventually told me was just a really good friend—and
Then he snuck away for days to see her, stealing kisses and much more

Than he said in a hotel room where we had once stayed—I would
Need to be patient, he said, like Penelope while she waited for Odysseus'
Return—most days he gave our marriage a seventy percent chance,

He was more than halfway sure that our life together would endure—
One solstice morning, the longest day of the year, he explained that,
By that evening he would know whether or not he would be returning.

When he called to say he was coming home—but first he wanted to
Invite her to have dinner with our family—and I said yes only because
I was so shocked—I was so happy that I cried—later that summer, we

Took a trip to Nova Scotia where he picked out a new quilt for our
Bed—it cost over a thousand dollars, more than I wanted to spend—
But he insisted, saying it was an important symbol of our recommitment

To one another—like our own private marriage renewal—every morning
I spread it carefully over the comforter on our maple bed—smoothing
Out the wrinkles—the one red square in the middle a symbol of our hearth.

Rotting Potatoes

Opening the drawer beside the sink, the divided one I loved on our first tour
Of our new house—almost five years ago now, to the day—I smell a moldy
Odor,
Potatoes decaying, their white sprouts pushing through the plastic bag—and

For an instant I cannot remember how old these tubers are—I can't recall
The last time I bought potatoes—and then it comes to me that it was Labor
Day—
That awful weekend when I was searching for normalcy, inviting friends over

For a meal while my husband explored another life altogether with a woman
Half his age, far across the country—I remember the date because he left
The receipt for his romantic dinner on the counter—it was only then

That I learned the limits of what no woman or man should ever have to bear.

Burberry Shirt

Yet again a stickler for veracity, my husband is proud to tell
Me again that he is washing his own clothes. I cry outright
When I see that he chose to wear his favorite blue and white

Striped shirt, one we bought together on a weekend in Maine—
To impress his new date. I rub my fingers against the fabric—
It is still too hard to believe for how long I have been deceived—

I know he must leave before there is nothing left of me.

Ritz Carleton Bar, Boston

How fast we ran away from our wedding reception,
How tightly we held hands on that hot July afternoon already
Fading into twilight—my dad had said it was rude for the bride

And groom to overstay their welcome—and so we ran along
The curving driveway to the waiting car while our guests threw
Birdseed at us instead of rice—

How we laughed when my husband
Signed the guest register for the first time: Mr. and Mrs. X—
How after we checked in, we went downstairs to the bar—perhaps

What I remember most was the beauty and gravity of his voice
When he raised a glass of whisky to his lips and said
'Here's to us, to forever,' later we kissed to seal our words.

Sidewalk, Ann Arbor

Very shortly after he proposed—he took a picture of me
Standing, caught in the autumn sunshine of an Ann Arbor afternoon—
So happy to have been chosen—and so was he, the luckiest

Guy in the universe, or so he said—hard to remember that he signed
Every card he gave me, *Love always* including the very last one
He handed me on our twenty-third anniversary—just one month

After he had been blinded by love for another woman.

A Cafe near Chartres

The weather here on this first day of the New Year is cold and we are sad,
A drizzle beginning this morning has turned first to sleet and then to snow—
After a chilly excursion to the Eiffel Tower we rush to see the cathedral—

Taking the metro for free, on the off chance my husband's mood may lift, for
This
Entire trip he has been glowering, glum, irritable, short-tempered. When I
Think back on his expression as he sat across from me sipping onion soup
and tea

I probably could have guessed he was plotting how to flee our nest, how to
Hide
The seeds of his duplicity; at the same time he was vowing
He would never leave, he was shouting how our life was simply not enough
for him.

Dancing School

Every morning I eat breakfast with my father and he makes me a soft-boiled
Egg, I ask him questions about Vietnam—the body count, the assassinations—
I recount the bomb scares we have at our school almost weekly—the ones where

The Cambridge fire department comes and we all line up and troop out
 To the far field to wait until the principal declares the all-clear
How dangerous that time seemed to me, and to my father—

Who forbade me to go on my own to Harvard Square—the older brothers
And sisters of my friends tripped, did LSD, dodged the draft—my
Mother and father fretted over me, trying so hard to keep me free from harm.

They sent me to dancing school with my best friend, S—it was on Thursday
Afternoons in the gym—we changed into our black velvet dresses and donned
Our white gloves before we walked out to meet the boys—they formed one

Line and we another—where we waited to be put into pairs for sets of waltzes,
Foxtrots, and the occasional tango—mostly we were not good enough dancers
What I remember from those days: the fear of being left alone, of being unchosen.

Driving to Lewisburg

Six o'clock on this October Saturday morning, the fields are frosty—
An Amish man slips out from behind a grove of red sumac to wheel
His bicycle down the road—his black hat square against mist rising

Between mountains—his presence reminding us we live in a valley
Where pastures are beside hills—where green lines come in rows
Of grass and corn—if I breathe deeply, I can still remember the way

My son's tiny hands fluttered inside me, fidgeting—always letting me
Know he was there, and would always be—now that same boy is almost
Grown, slumped beside me beneath a blanket, sleeping anywhere,

The way only teenagers can—I reach over and poke a hole for his breath.

Jet Trails

I am in the kitchen washing breakfast dishes when I look up and
See jet trails spreading across blue sky—pink sun streaking these
Mechanical leavings, like white lines chalked on a board—

Crisscross applesauce, a rhyme our children used to say—all the
Sundry journeys my husband took when I had no idea
Where he was going—or who he was with—it has now become so clear

What I could not see: he was leaving behind his own trail of lies.

Blood Tests

My family doctor has been kind. His office was the first place
I turned after my husband twisted my heart into a knot and
I thought there was something wrong with my stomach, deep

Inside. I couldn't keep anything down—the sight or
Smell of food repulsed me—he said there was nothing amiss
With my digestive track; instead I was having a stress reaction to

Grief—that's what he wrote on my chart—the doctor said it might
Take months, or even years before my head would clear,
Before I could expect to feel like myself again.

Eventually, he said, I should get tested for sexually transmitted
Diseases and AIDS, a precaution he would prescribe for any woman
In my situation. As I sat in the university clinic having my blood

Drawn, I thought of the joyful stings to our fingers
Years ago, one last chore remaining before our
Marriage license could be issued—and now it seems, I am waiting

To make sure that the only damage inflicted has been to my heart.

November

In November the branches continue to empty, nothing will keep the
Leaves on trees—every morning when I wake I find more have
Fluttered to the ground—as I have tumbled further into my new life—

The pear trees are almost bare—this time last year we had already
Had at least one blizzard—our whole family had dragged broken
Branches out to the curb with our bare hands until our backs ached

From exertion—now I will let the leaves fall where they may.

Twenty-Three Years and One Month

Standing in our kitchen, my husband reaches for the flour container
I am about to take our son to the dentist,
August days are filled with the mundane chores of love—

'I've booked a trip to: Albuquerque,' is what my husband says to me—
He has timed his announcement as though he is speaking to a group
Of dutiful students who will not respond;

We have been this way before and he has promised me,
Just as I have promised him, that each of us
Is all in—I follow him to the freezer where he stores the yeast—

And he pushes my arm out of the way—I have the sickening sensation
This time I cannot stay—still, I persist—it is, after all, our family's
Entire existence we are talking about—'Not a good time,'

He repeats, 'Not a good time.'

Mockingbird's Song

Like a mockingbird's song gone wrong, my husband cannot stop calling me—
For matters large or small, he does not seem to understand how much
I do not want to hear from him. I want him now to leave me alone

So that I can embark—I do not want to listen at midlife
To his lies, or truths, or anything else. He has confessed, recanted, and
Confessed again so many times I have no idea how to distinguish what

Was really my life and what it might have been. Still, he ruffles his feathers,
Rearranges his plume, and sharpens his beak. I realize the only way I can
Get his words out of my head is to stop answering the phone.

Shadow Builders

They come to work in darkness, before late dawn on these November
Days—when I look out my bedroom window, I see a few slim angular
Men climbing ladders, their straw hats tipped rakishly against our industrial

Age—when we returned from our last vacation as a family, we found a hole
Had already been dug in the vacant lot behind our house—dirt piled so high
We could no longer see the sky—the grass where our kids used to run bases

Long gone—all through this dreary autumn my marriage has been
Disintegrating
I have watched a tall white house come into view—hoping that the family
Who will move in soon might make a better go of it than we have done.

Reclamation

Piece by piece—I reclaim my life—new sheets, nightgowns, name.
I trade in my rings for a single band of diamonds, a promise ring I call it, marking
My vow that I will never allow myself to be treated

Poorly again—I don't want anything my husband purchased to touch my skin—
That last time we were together in this bed felt like rape.
Box by box I remove what was once his or ours from this house where

He once promised to live peacefully.

The Bucket

In times of crisis my husband reaches for metaphors—
Straining language to make sense of what cannot be sensible—

How many times he has twisted Donne's famous idea connecting
The arc of lovers to a compass to explain the presence of
Two women in his life, always another who is drawn to

Him by the infinite pull of the universe—
Always another who by one rotation of earth
Can change everything—he who stood and watched as

I almost bled out in the operating room after giving birth
To our children—almost lost my uterus, and perhaps my life

My blood overflowing buckets at the end of my bed.

After the First Lie

I don't know when it was that my husband began to lie, how could I—
He was so good—I suspect, like most occurrences in marriage,
It came to pass slowly, a series of accretions over the months and the

Years until it became a second nature, until it became so familiar
That perhaps even he did not know when he was lying and when he was
Telling the truth—despite the total chaos he has unleashed upon our

Lives, a sweet relief comes knowing I will not have to listen for his lies again.

Weeping Cherry Tree

We tore out scrub brush and seeded a new green lawn, filled
With exuberance and hope for where we had made our new life—
The sampling we had chosen arrived by truck, roots gathered

In a burlap ball—when we arrived home that sunny September
Afternoon, there it was—a weeping cherry tree ready to grow
Taller than any of us, to remain here long after we have all left

This earth—our daughter remarked that the thing looked as though
It belonged on a desert island, that's how scrawny it was—it
Resembled a miniature palm tree, she said—and in the five years

We have lived here it has, of course, grown and begun to blossom—
After the first rough winter when our dogs tried to dig it up—
Fascinated with the smell of soft dirt—on this November morning

The branches hang empty, spindly, desolate, waiting for winter.

Oysters

We sit across from the Arc de Triomphe, gleaming
At night, red car lights streaming around the traffic circle—Paris is
Lovely this autumn—and we have arrived to renew our love—

My husband has confessed. I have forgiven him, we have both vowed
To leave the past behind, to look ahead, to taste every oyster we can—
We make love many times a day—we lie in bed saying we cannot believe

How lucky we are to have made it this far—his transgression, his moods
And my resulting sulks—these are the variables we have argued over—
No more we say. He refers to what happened as a wake up call, a notice

That neither of us was paying enough attention to our marriage; he
Reiterates it was both of our faults, both of us were caught looking the
Other way. No more we say, No more, and everything seems possible

On that warm night when we shake salt and pour horseradish on these
Delicate creatures from every beach along the coast of France—

'*Dix huitres*' you repeat, ten—five for each of us—I think you may have
Given me a sixth. Now I know everything that evening was only for show.

Detrimental Reliance

A friend who's a lawyer once informed us of a term called detrimental
Reliance—a complex way of saying what happens when someone decides
Something based on false or incomplete information

It came in handy when we found ourselves involved in a dispute with our
Contractor. We were in for a nasty surprise—we were only saved from this
Mistake
By a slip of paper I'd stuck in a drawer with the project manager's errant
scribbles

In red, circling "on budget and on time." I have been
Practicing a form of detrimental reliance on my own. Would I

Have stayed the last ten years if I'd known the real truth?

My honest answer is I really don't know.

Plane Trees

Plane trees drop their yellow leaves along this wide avenue
As we stroll side by side—unsteady with jet lag and exhaustion, subsumed
With the harsh sexuality of our renewed love for one another—

I tell myself there is no way my husband will continue to lie—
After all, we have told each other everything—each of us has come
Clean in our hearts, with our disappointments and our expectations—

What marriage is perfect, I ask myself—none that I can think of—
It's all about making mistakes and forgiveness—my husband has
Forbade me to tell anyone about his almost affair—in return, I

Have asked him to promise me no longer to contact her—
Readily, he has agreed—I can recall a distinct moment of memory
As we walked along, holding hands, even though he didn't really

Like to, it was a concession, he said, that he was
Making to me—that, if he were not telling the whole truth, then
I would have given everything I had to a losing cause—

I blinked; it would not happen that way, he told me never again.

My Wedding Dress

Sweet Nymph and Open Sea

Meanwhile he lives and grieves upon that island
In thralldom to the nymph; he cannot stir,
Cannot fare homeward, for no ship is left him,
Fitted with oars—no crewmen or companions
To pull him on the broad back of the sea.
        —The Odyssey, Book V (Fitzgerald)

I saw no irony in the name of the designer who fashioned my
Wedding dress—no irony in purchasing my gown at a store
Called Calypso, also on an island—in this case, Bermuda—

It was a simple, cotton eye-lit lace mid-calf length garment—
Bought on the whirlwind of my last vacation with my parents
Before I married—we hopped a bus on a humid August noon—

In town, my father persuaded me to take a peek inside this store
Where he thought there just might be something for me—I tried
The white dress on for all of five minutes, size 6 fit me perfectly—

No alternations needed—I clutched the pink bag decorated with
Gold letters describing the goddess of temptation who persuaded
Odysseus to tarry long listening to her ambrosial songs until wiser

Heads prevailed and he set forth again on his long-delayed journey
Home where his wife Penelope was waiting for him—once he displayed
His knowledge of the trick of the bed, and his faithful dog, Argus,

Recognized him, then love was put to rights, a marriage restored,
Domestic tranquility preserved—I drew comfort from the simplicity
Of my wedding dress—it symbolized my confidence that I knew

What I was doing as I stepped down the red-carpeted aisle towards
My beaming husband-to-be, steadied by my father's arm—I believed
We loved each other with all our hearts—and so I could promise

To love for better for worse, for richer for poorer, in sickness and
In health—I believed we could sail through whatever storms life
Held in store for us—whatever journeys we undertook, it would

Be the two of us together, forever—all marriages must endure,
Sometimes less, sometimes more, if they are to last—my maid
Of honor tied and then retied my sash, a last minute dash to find

Something blue—a handkerchief from someone's pocket, her
Initials embroidered in turquoise—my father appeared with a
Shiny sixpence for my shoe—brought back from his last trip

To London—even though I knew he had his doubts, he granted
Me the dignity of a beautiful wedding day—there would be no
Hesitating now—we walked slowly up the stairs to wait in the

Vestibule for the trumpet voluntary to begin—he whispered
In my ear that he hoped the sixpence would bring me luck—
My father, ostensibly the least sentimental of men—offered

Me this promise of good fortune, this token with its beveled
Edges that I had tucked away in my jewelry box—just the other
Day I found it beside the pregnancy sticks that had turned blue,

Notes addressed to the tooth fairy, a purple and green bracelet
My daughter made in third grade for Mother's Day—
The hospital tag I wore on my wrist the day our twins were born—

The tiny anklet identification—his own lojack we joked—for
Our youngest son, his name and number matching mine—
For years, my wedding dress hung at the back of my closets—

As we moved from graduate student apartments and then from
House to house until one April morning when my husband told
Me he was no longer sure whether he loved me—I knew in my

Heart he was acting differently—there was a dissonance between
His words and his actions—a gap I couldn't explain as I saw the sun
Fall across his face beside our bedroom window—we were not

Where he wanted us to be, not after fifteen years of marriage then—
That was news to me—I stayed awake night after night as he flew
Around the country assuming I knew where he was and what he

Was doing—how wrong could I be—but at the time all I could think
To do was take my wedding dress to the Quality Dry Cleaners
Where I brought his shirts every week—after all, they promised

Love and memories preserved forever.

Eight years later, five hundred miles away, legally separated—I reach to
The top shelf of our cedar closet and grab the white box—I clutch the plastic
Handle to pull it down to the ground, smoothing over the pink receipt

I note the salient facts: I took the dress to the cleaners on the
Twenty-third of April, Shakespeare's birthday—I remember a clerk
Telling me the lace had yellowed some, they would do their best

But they might not be able to make it pristine again—I said that was
Alright with me—in her rounded hand, she pressed hard and wrote
In loops: 1 wedding gown: clean and preserve—she gave me a paper

To sign accepting the risk that it might not come entirely white
Again—even then I knew I was only trying to stem the damage—
The receipt says it would cost $110 dollars, requiring a minimum

Deposit of $75 to begin the work—the total coming to more than half
Of what the dress itself had cost—my father liked to brag that he had
Found me a beautiful wedding gown, but it had not broken the bank.

Never cheap, he did not mind finding a good bargain—my daughter
Used to wonder aloud when she looked at the pictures from our
Reception why my dress had not had a train, why it had been so plain—

She was sure, even at seven years of age, that she would want a
Fancier wedding than her father and I had—I think it is safe to
Assume she will not want to wear my dress—nor, I think, would I

Have wanted her to—some decades later, I haul
The white box containing my wedding dress to the Saint Vincent
De Paul store where I hope it may give another woman a chance

At happiness—after I drive away from leaving the box just inside
The back door, plastic handle still intact—I return home in the rain only
To have my husband call to ask if he can move back in again—

I know then the only answer I can give to his question.

Trash Day

The pear tree leaves rustle and swirl down around me
As I heave our trash out to the curb—this used to be
One of those chores we argued over—my husband

Claimed it was one of the many heavy burdens he had to
Carry, part of a suburban existence that made him feel
Confined, shackled, restrained from whatever it was

He so yearned to do with his life—I tried to get up early,
To beat him to the task so that he would not become the
Angry bear who raged, cursed, and complained—what he

Insisted was only a minute of passing temper—as I lug
The blue barrels that have followed us through seven moves
Gratitude fills me as I think of the peace of this, our first

Thanksgiving on our own—the peace of accountability,
Predictability and love—I cannot claim it doesn't also contain
Loss, but so also does it mean serenity and kindness will reign.

My children and I cook a beautiful turkey all together.

Spode

Roughly twenty-four years ago we sold off duplicate copies of our books—
Which together weighed more than our compact station wagon—as well
As duplicate posters, blankets, toasters—so that we could set up housekeeping—

A phrase my father used for cohabitation, something he did not believe should
Ever happen before marriage—it was August, I believe, perhaps early
September—
The air was soft and sweet—as I unloaded box after box I thought about what

Might lie ahead for us—I pictured buying a house one day. A quiet leafy street
In some university town where we would both become professors, and
Children would come our way—my husband remembered a teacher from college

Who had described a long and happy marriage as old china, chipped
And nicked, but loved not less rather more for all the imperfections—
How could I not imagine all our years any other way—

So happy I was, so secure in the belief we were soul mates—
As my husband declared in his toast to me—he said he loved me more than life
Itself—and this I believed from the man who inscribed the first book he ever

Gave me, *A Death in the Family* by James Agee: "the truth will set you free."

The Nightmare

I used to have a recurring dream, the only one I remember
That my husband did not really love me— not quite enough—
We were almost married, but I always woke up before the ceremony's

Completion. Afterwards, I would wake shaking, fearing I was falling
And, if he were there, my husband would hold me and whisper in my ear
That I was only imagining foolishness. My fears had no logical root.

He said my dream was yet another phantom birthed by my overly active
Imagination—nothing to do with the truth. We would lie together in bed
And he turned the universe around on me, explaining that the reason

I had the dream was because it was I who hadn't really married him
In my heart. He set me wondering until the next time I awoke
Shuddering, somehow aware of the lies I always knew were there.

Sleigh Bed

Shakespeare insulted his wife by leaving her his second best bed.
The indignity of his bequest
Makes more sense to me now—
I can no longer bear to sleep in the bed
My husband left behind—it has become a symbol of the worst of our
Life together and also the beauty it did contain.

Odysseus and Penelope knew one another by the puzzle contained in bed.
On a gray November day I visit a furniture store.
The saleswoman fans out a deck of cards for me to choose my discount from—
I scratch off the silver circle with a nickel to reveal the number beneath—

It turns out I have been lucky and received almost half off a display model.
She assures me this mahogany queen sleigh bed will be delivered and
Assembled in my bedroom by the first of December.

Leaving the Forest

Three months to the day my husband moved out, our youngest son's
Birthday—everything in my life is different now—some things better,
Others worse. I am coming to know my own mind again, to follow my heart,

To speak in my own words—for years I was wandering in dark and tangled forest,
Not knowing whether to turn east or west, until I came to a house inhabited
By a wicked witch who leaned out her window to taunt me, and she did not
Stop

Until one autumn morning I realized I was perfectly capable of leaving.

Heather Corbally Bryant (formerly Heather Bryant Jordan) teaches in the Writing Program at Wellesley College. Previously, she taught at the Pennsylvania State University, the University of Michigan, and Harvard College. She received her A.B. with honors in History and Literature from Harvard where she received the Boston Ruskin Prize for her thesis, "Sight and Sensibility: A Study of Praeterita." She received her PhD in Modern British and Irish Literature from the University of Michigan where she was a Regents Fellow. She has won outstanding teaching awards from Michigan, Harvard, and most recently, from Penn State.

Her academic publications include, *How Will the Heart Endure: Elizabeth Bowen and the Landscape of War*, (University of Michigan Press, 1992). This study of the relationship between war and literature was awarded the Donald R. Murphy Prize for best first book. In addition, she has assisted in the research for the Cornell Yeats Series as well as publishing articles on Bowen, Yeats, O'Faolain, and T.S. Eliot. She has given papers at international conferences and was a plenary speaker at the centennial celebration of Elizabeth Bowen held at University College, Cork, in 1999.

Beyond her academic publications, Heather Corbally Bryant has published a novel, *Through Your Hands* (2011) which received an Editor's Choice and Rising Star designation. Finishing Line Press published her first poetry chapbook, *Cheap Grace,* in 2011. In addition, she has published poems in *The Christian Science Monitor* and the 2007 anthology of poetry, *In Other Words*. The Parallel Press Poetry Series of the University of Wisconsin Libraries published *Lottery Ticket*, her second chapbook in 2013.

She has given readings at The Pennsylvania State University, The University of Wisconsin at Madison, The University of Illinois at Chicago, Southern Florida University in Ft. Lauderdale, Webster's Bookstore, State College, Folio Bookstore, San Francisco, the Palmer Art Museum in State College, and in Donegal, Ireland, Wellesley College, Notre Dame, Georgia Tech in Atlanta, and New York University. *Compass Rose,* her third poetry collection was published by Finishing Line Press in May 2016. *My Wedding Dress* is her first full-length collection of poetry. *Thunderstorm*, her second full-length volume, will be published by Finishing Line Press in the summer of 2017.

www.ingramcontent.com/pod-product-compliance
Lightning Source LLC
Chambersburg PA
CBHW070551090426
42735CB00013B/3149